Words from the Editors

"*Blooming Beyond the Boundaries* has clear thematic divisions of Khaotic's journey of growth thus far — in a way that makes you question whether you should or shouldn't be peering into a story that isn't your own.

It's like watching the empty community garden bounce back from a dry gray winter into a lush vibrant green invitation of life and resurgence. From visions of childhood heartbreak and indifference to the rough in-between of lessons learned that most (including myself) would agree should never have been in the curriculum to begin with, and lastly to learning and welcoming intentional love in all its forms and invitations.

The only difference being, Khaotic now knows how the lover should appear and what must be brought as an offering to gain access into the garden of her creation."

- Adam Guzman (@urbano.natgeo.osito)

"I'm usually very selective of the books I choose to read, and more often than not, they're some sort of fantasy or horror or epic romance that whisks me away to another dimension.

I almost never feel inclined to read poetry, and yet I finished *Blooming Beyond the Boundaries* in one sitting. This book isn't about taking you to another reality, it's about making you feel safe in the one you're in.

As a brown Muslim woman, I am forever grateful to Khaotic for revealing the broken parts of herself and showing us how to piece them back together."

- Nahrin Mahmud (@ohmygodshammy)

"As a follow up to *Plucking Petals of Poetry*, *Blooming Beyond the Boundaries* is a sensational piece of work. Grounding yet elevational, Khaotic has managed to embody what it is to find the light within yourself even while battling your darkest moments."

- Jahmadi Riascos
(@flipped.florals/@jahmadisworld)

"*Blooming Beyond the Boundaries* - a collection in which Khaotic bares a part of her soul to share with us her journey in becoming the woman I know her to be today.

In this book, Khaotic discusses the trials and tribulations she faces within her own family, the hope she finds within her friends, and how she's learned about love and heartbreak through her partners, all while navigating this world as she slowly starts discovering her identity as a Bengali American woman. While having the pleasure of reading her work, I discovered that there is more to her than what meets the eye and will continue to look forward to her future works as they reveal the many sides to her yet to be discovered."

- Ayesha Hena (@simplyesha9)

Blooming Beyond the Boundaries

KHAOTIC

Published by House of Khaos
Brooklyn, New York City

Cover Design by Kristal Morfa

My Gratitude Belongs To...

My chosen family.

Without whom I would not have found
the courage to share my story.

Table of Contents

I Begin

With a breath.
Facing the east side of my bedroom,
waiting for the Sun to kiss me.

With my mother's hands
weaving blessings into my hair.

On shaky feet, constantly moving,
no matter the pace.

Surrounded by all the goodness
I put out into the world, hoping
for it to meet me on its way back tenfold.

I begin at the edge of my yoga mat,
even on the days when *shavasana*
feels like the only place I want to be.

At the top of every blank page,
waiting for a poem to rid itself of me.

With a cup of *laal cha* to warm me
all the way down to my toes.

With a prayer to the universe,
to God if He's listening.

With a hope that just beginning is enough.

kintsugi.

I tell my mother
that I'm still in my bed with my sorrow,
lie there and try to pretend
my heart doesn't feel heavier than my eyes.

maybe if I could give this sadness a name –
show her how it adorns itself
with all my self-doubt and brings home a lover
that looks too much like my guilt,

then it might not be so difficult to talk
about how I struggled to breathe
under the weight of their affair.

my mother says to bow my head
and find my comfort in God.

I do not tell her that,
for now – God leaves me
with more questions than answers.

there are moments
when I catch a glimpse of myself
and muse about His sense of symmetry.

does He know that He hung my smile
a little higher on the left side of my face?
does it make Him chuckle
when He checks in on me?

if He checks in on me.

I look at my uneven smile and decide
that I am the oldest stranger I know.

most mornings begin as a new battle, a fight
to love a mind that refuses to love me back.

some days, I stand on the tips of my toes,
turn my face towards the sun,
and wish myself to be more than this feeling.

I wait for the rays of light
to find the hidden shadows of my darkest self
and wonder what will rise from them.
wonder if the next time I face myself in the mirror,

I'll find wildflowers blooming
through the spaces between each rib
and see that something beautiful could grow

from the pieces of me
that have long felt too broken to love themselves.

sometimes, I'll try something a bit more dangerous
and let myself hope –

that, eventually,
everything is bound to come together.

I will have found some way
to mend all these chaotic fragments.

maybe they'll stitch themselves into a map,
leading me to the parts of myself I have yet to meet.

but when I finally find the woman I am meant to be,
I hope that I can open my arms

and welcome her home.

11:11/make a wish

an Oreo ice cream cake three days after my birthday. my
unborn cousin doing backflips along my spine from the
inside of *choto fufu's* belly. three months later – a pregnant
pause, a collective holding of breath as doctors race to
save them both. the sound of *boro fufu's* scream shattering
the air, crying for the son her baby sister did not have
the chance to meet. for the mother her nephew would
always look for over his shoulder. the smell of
sandalwood amongst running rivers of tears as we say
goodbye to the woman who loved me like her own. a
shift in the ground beneath me, opening a chasm in the
earth. a void in my own heart that I have yet to climb out
of.

Dearly Beloved

We are gathered here today
to mourn the parts of me that have died
on the way to my becoming.

Here to give a moment of silence
for the seven year old looking for her mother
amidst the storm that disrupted her family.

To grieve the eleven year old who met depression
hiding under a veil at her aunt's funeral.

Please join me in a prayer for the fourteen year old
who was looking for comfort and found its look alike
in the hands of a boy with words bigger than his actions.

Plead loud enough for God to be listening
when we ask for peace for the eighteen year old
who lost her faith –

In Him,
in love,
in herself.

Let us grant forgiveness to the twenty-one year old
who left her lover with only half of her lonesome –
the other half remains with him.

Find grace for the twenty-three year old
who took too much of the world in her hands at once.
Who lost herself at rock bottom enough
to find a home there.

We are gathered here today
to mourn the parts of me that have died
on the way to my becoming.

Speak with kindness over the grave
of all these tender pieces of my heart.

Pray that the earth holds me in its warm hands
as I return to it and shows me
how to be born again when the time is right.

Fairy Tale with Laryngitis
and Resignation Letter
erasure poem after Jehanne Dubrow

You remember
her tongue
          a knife-cut with
    what escape   means.
          you write,
         this letter
             Your body
is a ship of pain. Pleasure is

         faraway.
you write

         witches, a prince in love
with the surging silence of women,
            You write
        these years
in   infinite oceans

    Sometimes
      you've been   the
shell of your heart

কানিজ

There's a little girl hiding under my lower left rib.

She writes me letters every few days,
subtle reminders of her nuanced existence.
I don't know how to comfort her,
how to console her through her grievances.

Instead, I drown her words out – pretend
my laugh is louder than the storm she rages.

I write her name on me still, a morbid reminder
of the things I could not run from.

Sometimes I wonder if I did nothing
but mark the grave of an old dream,
a distant memory.

But this body has felt like a graveyard
for far too long for another ghost to settle itself
in the space between my ribs.

So, I start to write her back.

Ask her about her dreams,
both the good and the bad.

Tell her that where we are now,
the sun shines more than it rains.

And even still, we learn to love the smell of the earth
after the sky unburdens itself,

like new beginnings and unrepentant cleansings.

I hold my hand out to her, ask her to trust
that I am becoming who she's always needed –

a listening ear, a guiding hand, a lighthouse
on the days that the waves threaten
to pull her beneath the darkness.

And so, it becomes
that we weather the bad days together.

Warm our palms around a cup of ginger tea,
and release regrets into the secret of the night.
Hug our sorrow like an old friend
before walking it to the door,

and remember to leave it open just a crack,
for it is only so long before joy
comes knocking again.

A Letter to Third Culture Children...
So, I Suppose, Another Letter to Myself

More often than not,
you are going to feel like a burden

perched on the shoulders of all the relatives
who worked hard at getting you a life
in the land of opportunity.

They will remind you once on your twelfth birthday
and once more on your eighteenth
that despite your body being born on this soil,
your soul began in your father's land.

Upon hearing this, you will struggle
to equate the word *home* with a village you've never seen
and people you've never met to have loved.

You are taught from a very young age
that everything is done for the sake of family.

You must walk with the pride of belonging
to a foreign nation.

You must speak with the accent your mother kept safe
on her tongue across the ocean.

You must carry yourself in a way
that does not bring shame to your father's name.

But how do you hold this weight with you?

With the heaviness of two clashing cultures
crushing down on your spine,
how do you not collapse into yourself?

In your parents' eyes,
life was meant to be lived in black and white.
Every decision had two roads and you were taught
to walk the one they themselves had followed.

The thought that you could ever lace up your boots
and pave a new path for yourself

was too far-fetched,
too dangerous,
too out of norm
for their society to accept.

So, let me be the one to say it.

It is okay to croon along with Adele
about heartbreaks you could only ever hope
to experience while finding comfort in a cup of *chai*.

Your rebel aesthetic in muscle tanks and leather jackets
does not diminish your beauty in a *salwar*.

Even though the timbre of your voice rings louder
than the four walls of your room can hold,
you must never silence yourself
to fit into a mold that wasn't meant for you.

The duality of your identity does not signify
the erasure of either of your halves.
Let the hyphen between Bengali and American
be the bridge that your parents are too afraid to build.

You exist.

In all your mismatched socks,
eyeliner as sharp as your mother tongue,
and oversized denim jacket glory,

you are here.

And that is as good a reason as any
to live however you want.

Ancestry

When my parents lament the loss
of a love and language they can only find
in the rich soil of my grandparents' backyard,

I close my eyes and wonder of the girl I could have been.

The girl I would have been
had they never found the courage
to relearn everything they knew
with a lifelong mouthful of broken ancestry.

In my village, trees taller
than the humble home where my roots begin
bore mangoes sweet enough
to bring a smile to my *Dada's* stoic face.

Dadu was always sneaking *paan*
under the drapes of her *sari*, like the evidence
of her mischief wouldn't paint her teeth red
the next time she tried to grin
her innocence at me.

My mother's still soft hands use a rolling pin
to perfect the *roti* for breakfast,
while the vegetables from my father's garden
sizzle on the stove next to her.

I am sitting under *Dada's* watchful eye,
waiting for him to begin lazing under the sun,

in hopes of sneaking away to skip rocks
in the river twenty steps from our home.

Dadu sits on the cot behind me, and we listen
as the birds color the skies with their songs.
Her weathered hands start separating
the strands of my hair, the musky scent
of amla oil permeating the air
as she runs her fingers along my scalp.

I smile as she bickers with *Dada,* teasing him
about the surly shape of his mouth, despite
the warmth we all know of in his words.

My mother brings breakfast to the family room
and we sit in a circle –
cross our legs, and follow along
as my grandparents lead the *bismillah* over our plates.

My mother places my favorites in front of me
while my father glows about his morning's crops,
promising me the best of the squash,
the pumpkins, the eggplants.

I take a sip of the fresh *lassi* and fill my belly
with the feeling of family, knowing that

in this world, I am loved wholly,
and without question.

Herkimer Street

My first home smelled like green apples
and the soft breeze coming in
from our Bed-Stuy backyard.

My mother spent most mornings in a kitchen
too small for the size of her heart
as she kneaded *roti* dough for family breakfasts.

When New York winters beat
against the panes of our windows, we found warmth
under blankets big enough to take up their own suitcases
on their way in from Bangladesh.

Saturday nights were spent huddled in a living room
with my cousins as a Harry Potter marathon
took over the screen for a couple of hours.

In those moments, home was always a feeling.

Of waking up in the mornings and realizing
my favorite cousin lived in the apartment upstairs.

Of smelling the aroma of *chai* in the air
as my aunts and uncles speak of household affairs
still too political for me to understand.

Of sharing hearty dinners with my family,
cross legged on the kitchen floor
of our humble two bedroom abode.

But somewhere along the way,
home became a feeling I started to chase.

Looking for in the corners of the new bedroom
I've decorated with so much intention.
Behind the spices in the cabinet of my mother's pantry.
Between the folds of heavy blankets
that never seem to keep me fully warm anymore.

Until I realized that creating a home
is even more powerful than looking for one.

And so I build one for myself
with every poem that I write.
Use imagery and metaphors as brick and mortar
to house an open heart, and let myself
become the very home I was looking for.

An Insider's Guide:
Breaking Generational Cycles
in a Bengali Household

When your family stands behind the glass
of a one-way mirror and finds the audacity
to comment on the richness of your skin,

let them know what it feels like
to be loved so openly by the sun.

That the brown of your hands reminds you
of the earth from which you found
the courage to grow.

Do not ever allow your voice to be silenced
by a language that fought for its own right to be heard.

Speak your truths loud enough
to hide the colony of butterflies
you swallow before doing so.

Fuck the culturally conservative customs
that try to fit your feet into glass slippers.
Break into the rooms they work to keep you out of
and use your hands to shatter glass ceilings instead.

Dip the fragments in color
and frame the windows of your future home
in ways that only ever invite light into your life.

Dichotomy

My parents speak two languages,
and in neither one do they know how to say,
"I love you."

Instead, they knock insistently on my door.
Ask if I've eaten, sliced guavas already in hand
just in case I say no.

Once, in the fourth grade, I got sick with a fever
that left me in bed for seven nights.
And for seven mornings, my mother woke up
an extra hour early to slice the potatoes
for the *aloo bhazi* she knew I loved.

My father spent years turning my name on his tongue
enough for it to become another daily prayer –
covers me in God's grace every time I step outside.

On the evenings he falls asleep
before he knows I'm okay,
I hear him rustle awake not long after I walk in.

Shift in bed still half asleep and ask my mother
if I've made it in yet, as if the sound of me coming home
would always reach his ears.

There has never been any doubt
as to whether my parents love me –
only in if it will ever be enough.

When their sadness speaks to me before they do,
when their anger turns words
into weapons of careful destruction,

I struggle to believe that it will ever be enough.

My parents speak two languages
and in neither one do they know how to say,
"I'm sorry."

Instead, they ask why we need to make amends,
like this love between us isn't something worth mending.
Too stubborn to realize that a single apology
could carry generations of trauma off my back.

I try to plead with them –
that any thought on how they raised me
is no attack on their character, no indication of failure
on their parts as humans only trying their best.

I wish to be better in this regard.

Hope that if my child were ever to walk up to me
and admit that my words left wounds I could not see,

then I would fold my hands in forgiveness
and shed my ego long enough to remember
that it was never about me.

Remember that my impact
would always eclipse my intention,
and so, this is where I need to pay attention.

Learn to apologize, learn to reaffirm –
learn to love in as many languages as possible

to give what I did not receive.

A Letter to My Traditional
Bengali-Muslim Mom

Mom.

When I get dressed in the morning,
the first thing I do is iron out the curve of my spine
and remind myself that good posture
is the mark of a good character.

My shoulders are meant to carry
Dad's respectable reputation
and your non-negotiable expectations

and while I try my best to wrap my hands
around the world that you deserve,
I can't help but worry that they are too small
to carry the one that you expect.

Mom.

I know you think that every line of ink on my skin
is another mark on my soul, so I promise you
that this body is only a canvas
for all the things that could not kill me.

But all these things that could not kill me
still made me want to die.
So instead, I turned each into a piece of art
and hoped that by hanging it on myself,

I could find something beautiful worth living for.

Mom.

In a world like this,
to be a woman is to commit a crime.
In a world like this, I am told to apologize

for speaking too loud,
for loving too hard,
for daring to take up space.

When I do these things anyway, I know you think
it is only because I like breaking the rules.

But if loving who I am is a crime in your eyes,
then you've condemned me to a lifelong commitment
of proving my innocence.

Mom.

Some days, I want nothing more
than to be everything you want.

The daughter who bows her head five times a day
to a God she has no qualms with.
The one who embraces the culture
you drape off every wall of your home.

But your daughter wants to know
why her God never seems to write her back.

Your daughter lives as the bridge
between Bengali and American.

Even after loving the way you taught her to,
giving more than she will ever let herself take,
your daughter breathes knowing you consider her
to be everything you could not get right.

Mom.

Do you know how much that breaks my heart?

Parallel Lines

Every Tuesday at five,
I sit across from my counselor and wait
as she settles in with a notebook and a pen.

The events of the last week spill
into the space between us,
and somewhere along the way,

we unearth the box of memories
that I've tucked into the furthest corner of my mind.

I learn to play Connect the Dots with my inner child –
tie my past to my present in a small attempt
to reshape my future.

As I talk,
Donna purses her lips in professional solidarity,
writes down notes for future clarity,
and when she looks at me and nods sympathetically,
I almost forget that trust is often a rarity.

But I do trust her.

So, when she invites me down the rabbit hole
of analyzing my relationship with my mother,
it's no surprise that by the eighth session,

I find myself
crying at all the things I knew but never said.

When I speak of my religion,
tell her how it stands between my mother
and unconditional love,

Donna asks me who I think she'd love
if religion did not hold her back.

It only takes a total of two seconds,
one in which I realize my answer,
and the second in which I wish I didn't.

> *"Me."*

Her pen stops moving,
and when she looks at me, I see the way
sadness shapes her mouth around her next question.

> *"You think your mother doesn't love you?"*

There's no humor in the quick grin
that comes and goes from my face,
a forced nonchalance in the shrug of my shoulders.

It takes a few seconds for me to speak,
and when I do,

it's with every ounce of strength to make sure
my voice doesn't break as quickly as my heart did.

> *"I think…my mother can only love me if I agree with her.*
> *That's the difference between us – is that I love her*
> *even if I don't agree with her.*

You see, my mother and I have learned
to swallow our sorrows and call it breakfast.
We drape our trauma across our collarbones
alongside our favorite gold necklaces
and trade teardrop earrings for those adorning our faces.

Nurture anger in our wombs, and give birth
to resilience in the face of every obstacle
meant to bring us to our knees.

But where I find comfort in control,
my mother has wanted to surrender.
Leave her fears in God's palms and trust
that she will only ever receive what is meant for her.

I have not yet learned
how to allow myself this kind of vulnerability.

I find contentment in the taste of coffee
and caramel on my tongue,
in the smell of the earth after it rains.

I sense belonging take root
in the feel of fresh soil between my fingers,
in the sound of my lover's laughter.

And when I see the blessings that surround me,
I remember to breathe gratitude for what is mine.

But I have never trusted the darker parts of my mind
with anyone but myself, and even still,
I remain wary of my own intentions.

How am I to then place my faith
in He who I cannot see?

Who cannot rest a hand on my head
when it bows under the weight of my tears?

Who cannot speak to me with reassurances
when fear and doubt make a home
in the hollow of my bones?

I write letters to God every few weeks
and remember to add a postscript.

Does He love me enough to ever write back?
Because if my mother can't love me without condition,
then why should I believe that her God can?

We walk through our lives, looking for the peace
that promises to be a balm to our weary souls.

The paths we take become the boundaries
that divide us as our beliefs fill the space
between her heart and mine.

And it seems improbable,
maybe even a little irrational,

to hope that one day
we may reach our hands out to each other,
lessen this chasm between us and meet

somewhere in the middle.

Inheritance

My mother takes her jewelry box out of the safe,
embroidered fabric weary and worn with the love
passed down from her mother before her.

Runs her hand along heavy gold necklaces
that have weighed on her neck
since the day she received them as a bridal gift,

as she grieves the legacy
she feels she cannot leave behind.

An inheritance of shame swallowed
in the name of family.
Of grief embraced in the name of love.

When my aunt reminds her of the day
she will inevitably have to give me away,
without a last name that wasn't even hers to begin with,
our eyes meet for a quick second.

She says, *"Well, of course.*
I'd give her everything I could —
if only she wanted it, if only she would accept it."

Pearls of Wisdom
from my mother

It is considered *sunnah* to smile.
Do it with warmth. And do it often.
It is the easiest act of kindness.

Giving to the lesser fortunate
will never lessen what you have

but will return blessings into your hands
in ways you can't imagine.

If there is a chance to forgive someone,
do not hesitate to take it.

Live your life with grace,
people will always remember you
for how you treat them, how you make them feel.

Keep your heart open, and lead with love.
It is the only way for you to honor yourself.

Wings

I first tasted home on my tongue
in the space between my mother's arms.
The trouble became that we were not
an affectionate family.

There was no abundance of kisses over skinned knees,
much less hugs to heal any broken hearts.

Love was cooked into your favorite meals
and served four times a day,
so, there was never enough room for question.

But somehow three unsaid words
wore an elephant's face and sat across from us
at the dinner table every night.

For a while now, I have been running,
and according to God's wicked sense of humor,
only ever in a circle.

Away from myself, and back towards a home
I could never fully settle in.

For my mother,
religion was packed neatly next to the culture
she carried in a suitcase across the ocean.

She left behind the familiarity of her language,
brought with her an accent

that is always a work in progress,
and a God that this world has deemed too extreme.

The walls of her house were marked with invisible ink,
the word *stranger* a glaring reminder
of what it costs to try and belong anywhere
other than where you are accepted.

And much like my mother,
I find myself branded as an outcast
in what is meant to be my home.

Searching for love outside of her language,
outside of her God,
outside of the gilded cage she has made of her arms,

so that maybe I could begin to find it
within myself first.

Mornings with Ma

My mother stocks her kitchen with spices
she saved from her mother's cabinets.

Turmeric, cumin, and chili
are non-negotiable for your pantry —
you need it for the base of almost every dish.

In the early light of weekend mornings,
I stand by her right side and wait patiently
to flip the *roti* she's prepared for everyone's breakfast.

Make sure your thaffa *is hot, only then is it ready —*
it will ruin your roti *otherwise.*

Some days, she shares stories of her childhood with me,
the aroma of *chai* brewing on the stove inviting
only reminiscence to her tongue.

The best kind of chai *comes from patience —*
nothing that's worth it ever will ever come easily.

When she adds the finishing touches
to my favorite *aloo bhazi,* my heart stutters
in childish excitement as the smell brings me back
to breakfast on the first day of fourth grade.

You need your strength if you want to do well in life,
and that begins with a proper meal in the morning.

She brings both plates of food to the table
in one hand, a lifetime of experience
in juggling more than one thing at a time.

The key to doing well in the kitchen is timing —
once you master that, you can succeed anywhere.

I set a coffee mug filled with her morning apple juice
by her hand and sit beside her
for the most holy part of my day.

Never take a bite of your food
without thanking God for your blessings,
it is gratitude that will continue to feed you.

She breathes a thank you to God
for providing for us,

I whisper a thank you to God for her.

Most Likely to Cry
for A New Leaf on Her Dying Plant

If there's anything of my father
that I can claim with a warm pride,
then it would be that he has more of a green arm
than a green thumb.

I've lived in three different apartments in my whole life,
and in each one, my father has made sure
to have a backyard of open space.
An oasis for himself, a home for the garden
he intended to nurture every time
the weather got warmer.

Some mornings, if I am awake early enough,
I notice him through the mirror of my window.
Watch as he walks around the yard,
a few intentional minutes spent with every plant
learning to grow.

He uses his palms to check the soil,
makes sure there is enough water to feed the roots –
a surprising tenderness to large hands
weathered down by years of labor.
Of building a home for his family.
Of trying his best to provide.

I thought he did it because it was easy.
Assumed that I could mimic his actions
after years of observing and learn to cultivate

lush green sanctuaries of my own.

But when I brought home my first marigold
from a school-trip, its wilting petals in a matter of days
told me that the jade hues on my hands
were as impermanent as the flower itself.

So I watch him again, not unlike
the way he watched his own father.

Learn more about what it means to be patient,
to allow things to grow in the season they are meant to.
Learn the balance between
what is too much care and what is too little.

And when I see a budding leaf
on the lonely stem of my struggling snake plant,
I smile to myself –
remember my father's green arms
and how much I have grown in them.

I Am My Father's Daughter

When my voice climbs up the notches of your spine,
it is only to reach for more love to fill you with.
To invite you into my laughter
by tickling you out of your own.

I am my father's daughter.

I love to watch the fruits of my labor grow taller
from the small pockets of earth I plant them in.
I have learned to use my hands to pour into others,
even when my own cup remains empty.

I am my father's daughter.

Sometimes, my anger gets the best of me.
Runs ahead of my understanding to stand watch
at my heart and I am unable to hold back
the bite of my guard dog tongue.

I am my father's daughter.

I know how to cut a piece of myself out
every time I see someone else may need it.
Or maybe even just want it.

Want me, I mean.

I am my father's daughter.

So, I hide my tears in the comfort
of God's oblivion to my pain – filled to the brim
with more feeling than I know what to do with.

Unable to admit that the only thing I need
is a hand, or a hug.

I am my father's daughter.

Unlearning everyday what I believe life should be,
trying only to accept the joy in that it is.

I am my father's daughter.
And how blessed I am because of it.

A Seat at the (Dinner) Table

My last Sunday afternoon was spent in a house
that once used to be home
to all the growing pains of my girlhood.

I shared *chai* in red plastic cups
with one too many cousins and all my aunts,
and the swirling taste of black tea and milk
brought me back to summer and childhood.

The former always passed by too quickly
to savor on my tongue,
and the latter I revisit during nights
shrouded in star-studded nostalgia.

My aunt's hand found the top of my head
in absentminded affection.
And, for a second, my voice trembled
as emotion took hold of my throat.

When she asked if I was okay, I smiled.
Told her I must be cold, and closed my eyes
to steal a moment and lean in.

I have exhausted so many birthdays
looking for a home within my family,
sometimes heartbroken in my certainty
that there wasn't one to begin with.

And yet somehow,
there is no doubting the care my aunt
cooks into my favorite meal
knowing that she has invited me over for lunch.

No denying the love in my uncle's voice
as he tells me about all the plants he's picked out for me.

It could only be belonging
that thread our hearts together
when my cousins throw their arms
over my shoulders to anchor me
on the days that I am floating.

I have exhausted so many birthdays
looking for a home within my family,
often forgetting that there is always a place

where someone chooses to make one.

Hello, God? It's Me, Khaotic.

I've found my way to the end of this life,
climbed out of the gentle embrace
of the earth's hands before realizing
the muddy footprints I've trekked up
the stairway to Your doors.

The tremor of my own hands feels like quakes
rumbling between my fingers as I knock hesitantly.

There used to be angels perched on my shoulders,
hiding horns under halos, insisting
that You could never love a sinner like me.

When all the letters I sent You
asking if it were true came back unanswered,
I took it to mean they were right.

Took it as a sign
that You didn't want to rest Your eyes on a girl
who couldn't see past her ego long enough
to put her faith in something bigger than herself.

I wonder now if I tried hard enough.

Did I pack my prayers
with enough good intention
before tucking them under Your windowsill?

Did I leave my pride at the door of the mosque
every time the *adhaan* called
and You asked me to show up as I am?

Have I asked forgiveness for all the times
You've left blessings in my palms
and I was too blind with arrogance to be grateful?

Have I learned to breathe grace
where I haven't yet been able to find it?

I have been convinced by so many
that You could never love a sinner like me.

But maybe my sin lies in the fact
that I believed what others would say
before I believed in You.

Believed that You would condemn me for my mistakes
before You could ever forgive me for them.

So, I stand before You today,
as humbly as the day You breathed life into me,
to ask You for one more chance.

Ask that this time,
if You can –

will You believe in me?

Revolutionary Grounding Reminder
for Brown Girls Like Me

They will question your goodness.
Make a mirror out of themselves
and stand in front of you hoping to see
everything that you want to keep
away from prying eyes.

Remember not to let shame grow
amongst this inspection.
Remember that anything worth protecting
is something worth saving.

They will doubt your resilience.
Use unforgiving hands to bandage
the cuts on your knees, while wounding you
even further with thinly veiled reminders
of your supposed weakness.

Like it doesn't say more that you chose to get back up.
Reach out for help in a culture
where it is likened to admitting failure.

Is the failure not in the way they choose not to see us?

Pass their eyes over our breaking backs
and convince themselves it is because
we do not bow down to God enough?

They will lack faith in your strength.
Your discernment, and your intelligence.
They will try to cloud all the dreams
you reach your hands out to the horizons for,

but I promise – it is not because
they do not believe in you.

But rather, they cannot believe
that you have pulled enough courage out of your veins
to bloom so beautifully beyond their boundaries.

Love Has Looked Like

the soft touch of my father's first kiss
on my furrowed baby brow

my grandfather's watchful eye as I found
childlike wonder under every rock in our village

understanding that my little brother
needed my mother more than I wanted her

watching my niece fill the universe with her first breath

the ground shifting beneath me
when my aunt left this earth after her last breath

wrapping myself in warm words of poetry
every time the weather got colder

the boy from Florida, with the pretty words
and a secret smile

my best friends by my side at the precinct,
holding my hands as I explained to the officer
why I didn't deserve it

finding trust in the coffee brown of my eyes,
no longer turning away from the girl in the mirror

growing into the parts of myself I hid from,
accepting of all the darkness
that inevitably comes to light

my chosen family surrounding me in surprise
on my birthday, a medley of hearts as grateful as mine
as we celebrate another year of being alive together

Reasons to Love Me

Because when I get my favorite tacos
on a breezy summer day, I do a happy dance
that I like to think no one can see.

Because my taste in music speaks more languages
than I do, but each of my favorite songs
still feel the same kind of blue.

Because I'm really shitty at remembering anything
other than almost every other line of The Office.

Because no matter how much my hands shake,
I have yet to fail at building myself back up.

Because sarcasm has found a voice in my wit,
and carved a home out of my smirk.

Because I could spend an entire day at a bookstore
and never complain. Or a museum. Or a park.

Because I wouldn't be complaining much
with you around anyways.

Because I try my best to hold onto simpler days
with a fistful of sunshine in one hand,
and a chocolate Mister Softee cone in the other.

Because I am intentional with my gratitude
for things as small as the jade plant
that greets me from my window every morning.

Because I have this thing where I can only enjoy
ice-cold water, even in the middle of a New York winter.

Because I am quite possibly the worst kind of poet –
too busy writing to feel, too busy feeling to write.

Because I like to leave little hearts next to the lines
that break mine in every new poem that I read.

Because I choose to believe that I know nothing.
And, as a result, I will question everything.

Because everything does not include us.
Because it never includes us.

A Letter to My Tattoos

Mom hates you guys.

I mean, there's really no sugarcoating it.
She's written you off as another attempt at rebellion –
like this is just a phase,
like this is something I'll get over.

I don't know if she knows how tattoos work.

I want to tell her about you.
How it all started when I was eighteen,
coming out of a love that controlled me too much
to ever let me feel in control.

Tell her the first tattoo was about flying on my own,
placed deftly on my right shoulder blade.
I'm terrified of heights, and even more so of needles,
but I laid in that chair for forty-five minutes
and found freedom in the pain that I fell into.

This I could control.

I want to show her the lotus on my sternum,
and my need to put art on top of a heart
broken one too many times.

Do you think she'll listen
to the inner child on my left rib?
See the regality in the Basquiat on my left shoulder?

Appreciate the years of friendship bound
in the pinky promise on my right side,
and the childhood innocence immortalized underneath?

I need her to know

that I welcomed the bite of her mother tongue
as I had the words *free soul* etched onto my hip,

a silent act of defiance against the language
that dared to try and hold my voice captive.

That every time the needle touched my skin,
another wound on my soul stitched closed.

That I felt more like a mosaic and less like shattered glass
with every piece of art that I hung on myself.

That I littered flowers all over my body,
only so that no matter which way I tilted my head,
my gaze landed on one

and I am reminded once again to bloom.

Blueprint to Being a Woman

They tell me I'm doing it wrong.
Show me a map of what they think
it means to be a woman –

the mountains of shame to hide between my legs,
the valleys of consent most cross without paying the toll.

My girlhood was only meant to teach me the blueprint –

how to cross my ankles just so,
enough for them to believe that I am demure.
Know that I am not leaving things open for invitation.

How to lower my gaze enough to play coy,
to look no one in the eye in case they see me
for who I am, and not for who they want me to be.

How to strip my voice of its resounding cadence
enough to seem feminine,
by which they truly mean docile.

My womanhood was never meant to belong to me.

Clutched instead in the fist of every man
trying to claim one more thing
that he has no right to.

Every attempt to take back what is mine
looks like sitting however I please,

no invitation unless I say so.
Looks like keeping my gaze steady,
like letting my voice ring.

My womanhood will always remain my own,
despite how often they try to convince me otherwise.

an ode to thick thighs.

when I was younger, my mother used to say
I was all skin and bones.

it was a wild thing to wrap my mind around
because I was never just skin and bones.

I was warmth
and love
and light
and magic.

as I grew older, she started to see what I meant
in the swell of my hips and the curve of my thighs.

she worried that the eyes that followed me
down the street would be preceded
by catcalls and wolf whistles.

evidently, there is nothing humane
about the way this society degrades its women.

there is nothing humane
about the way this society shames its women.

there is nothing humane
about the way this society fails its women.

on the days that the sun kisses
my skin with a little more passion,
I am warned not to wear anything too…much.

I wanted to smile and tell my mother
that the day I give two fucks
about who I am too much for,
I will have become too little for myself.

I have come to learn that the power in my walk
shakes the earth beneath me
but the only ones who are afraid
are those with unsteady feet.

I was raised with the notion
that I must look to others for validation
when in truth, I have held the universe inside of me
since the moment I took my first breath.

I am a woman.

and for far too long,
I have worn this title like an oversized sweater,
trying to shrink both the word and myself
to fit what society tells me I should be.

I should be seen and not heard.
I should speak when spoken to.
I should swallow my individuality

to protect the fragile ego
of the patriarchal dictatorship,

I mean "democracy",
we live in.

now, I roll up the sleeves of this behemoth sweater,
and let anyone who gets in my way know

that the only way I will be silenced
is if my body is laid down
in the same earth that it came from.

but until then,
I would wear the word woman over my shoulders
with the same pride a warrior wears their armor.

Rebel

What do I need to do?

Wake up and recognize your first conscious breath
as the first blessing of the day.

Wash your ideas of failure
off your shoulders from the day before
and wear renewed determination around your wrists.

There is a book waiting to be picked up by you,
waiting for you to take everything it is able to give.

Remember that a well-educated woman
is only the most dangerous kind.

What if I have my own things to say?

Brew a warm cup of tea –
add some cardamoms, a bay leaf or two, ginger,
and a healthy sprinkle of your favorite black tea leaves.

Sit by a window with the most sunlight
and wait to see what grows from the tips of your fingers.

Give yourself to your pen
and watch as the pages bleed with your voice.

What if they don't like what I have to say?

Say it again.
And again.
And again.

Until you realize that your truths are louder
than those too scared to accept them.

Declare that you are happy in your wholeness,
love and be loved in return by your own reflection.

What a blessing it is to belong to yourself.

How do I stay honest?

Allow yourself to break when the time comes.
Remember that the cracks in your spirit
are new spaces for growth, for life.

Smile at every stranger whose soul
you seem to recognize, maybe
they'll introduce you to the next part of yourself.

How do I change the world?

Speak, darling.

Your words are bigger than you,
bigger than this mold they will try to fit you in.

You were born with your mother's fire,
and her mother before her,
and her mother before her.

Do not feel alone in moments of weakness,
but instead, find your strength
in the stories of the generations before you.

You are here to be a beautiful rebellion.

Horoscope for a Precocious Pisces
February 18ᵗʰ – March 20ᵗʰ

When your therapist learns enough about you
by your sixth session to call you resilient,

do not feel the need
to doctor your expression into anything polite
before graciously refusing the compliment.

"Resilience is a painful virtue."

One you need not wear like some badge of honor
to justify your already weary voice at only 23.

If resilience is a virtue,
then God will forgive you
for wanting to be the unholiest of them all.

There is only strength in your softness.
Nothing but grace in your vulnerability.

So, wipe your lips of the shame
you have sugared them with since finding space
for yourself in her chair and recognize

how defiantly you have chosen to show up for yourself.

I Try to Write a Poem About My Anger
after Michelle Awad

And it comes out looking like
closed fists and measured breathing.

Sounds like lethal silence
because my anger lives in the hollow of my throat.
Creeps up to settle along the clenched lines of my jaw
and sits on my tongue, heavy and acrid.

Red hot pin pricks dance across every inch of my skin
when my anger builds a bonfire in my belly,

burning for the blood of every transgressor
to break my boundaries –
my anger rises like a phoenix from the ashes of my hope.

Demands for the better it believes I deserve
and tells me it is going nowhere
until I learn to fight like I believe it too.

Garden of Eden

My anger is a slowly rotting apple –
tempting me to take a bite

knowing that I am Eve's daughter.

Metamorphosis

I spent most of last night preparing myself
for the arrival of March.

As if the end of another journey around the sun
would somehow lure me out of the chrysalis
I have made of my room and trigger my rebirth
into the best version of myself so far.

Where all these things that I am –
a poet, a lover, a friend –
everything becomes more somehow.

Doesn't anyone get it though?

That what I also am
is heartbroken, lonely, exhausted.

Tired of every poem I write
being so damned sad, so fucking heavy.
These are the ones that find me the easiest,
and I have yet to know

why happiness hides from me
in the skeleton of every unfinished piece.

They say we're moody, us Pisces –
that we like to play damsel in distress.

I say it's hard to play the damsel
when I've had to be my own hero this whole time.

Disembodied

Much of my time has been spent
in looking for a home in this body.
Wondering if I'd ever feel as big as my smile
on the days the Sun holds my face in her hands.

Doubting that my own hands could ever be strong
if I couldn't even hold them steady.

I worried constantly that my legs would give out
before I could carry myself to where I needed to go.

Looked for love everywhere except my own heart,
because *fuck*, if it wasn't always aching.

But, dear body, I understand now
all that you have done for me,
so please forgive me for the time it took
for me to appreciate as much.

I am only now learning to be more intentional
with my gratitude towards you.
Recognizing the butterfly of a blessing
that every breath becomes.

There is too much to be uncertain of in this world,
and this is one of the few things of which I am certain.

So, dear body,
this letter will only be of soft thank you's.

For the pillar you make out of my spine,
keep my back straight and my head high
on the days the world sits heavy on my shoulders.

For the lullabies you create
from the anxious hummingbird in my chest,
teaching me to rest whenever my spirit turns weary.

For the love you still carry with your bleeding heart,
arms heavy with the weight of everything
you have yet to give.

For the evenings you spend tending to this poet
when all I've done is try to climb out of myself
with every poem I've ever written.

To My Longest Lover

I'm so sorry to have kept you waiting –
this has certainly been a long time coming.

I've been meaning to tell you for a while
just how much I love your lop-sided smile.

I love the way you glow
every time you read a good poem.
Even more so when you write a good poem.

I think it's beautiful that you never consider
pulling your hands back from those who need you.
Even if you need more.

My hope for you is that you always stay this way.

I want you to find your smile
even after you lose yourself under a stream of tears.
I want you to take the time and read all the good poems,
and to write all the great poems.

I think, more than anything, I want for you
everything you've always given others –
love, patience, kindness.

To accept these things with open arms
when they come your way,
as you deserve nothing less.

Ruminant
erasure poem after Clodagh Beresford Dunne

a heart

cannot bear to be seen.

bellows to the heavens,
again. And again.

There Is Nothing Beautiful

Tonight, I do not feel compelled to write.
Do not want for catharsis in the form
of tainted imagery and ruins of metaphors left behind.

Tonight, there is no ritual for how I bleed.
How I let this soft animal of a body exist in itself
with no means for escape.

Tonight, there is nothing beautiful
about the becoming of this poem.
In the grief that struck me before it,
or the anger that moves me after.

There is no rhyme.
No reason in this labyrinth of a mind.
No voice of reassurance that I will find my way out.

Tonight, there is only chaos.

Stage Fright

There are words I've never uttered, trapped
behind the confines of my lips.

I can't help but be terrified
of the day they riot against my silence,
realizing their need to be heard.

Maybe it's meant to be ugly,
this protest of emotion in my throat.

I couldn't dare call myself a writer,
the way these blank pages make me nervous now.

Puppeteer Poetry

I've been spending countless mornings
by the light of my window to open myself up,
not unlike the notebook in front of me.

Every breath becomes intentional as I exhale
the pride I've scraped from the insides of my throat.
Traces of it hide between my teeth as I write,
finds its way forward only when I say

that I must "pretty it up"
before I can call anything a poem.

Can you believe that?
The audacity of me to assume
that poetry cannot also be an ugly thing.

Something to grab me by the strings of my heart
and play puppeteer with my emotions.

I've had a lot of practice pulling the ugly out of me –
try to keep watering dead bouquets in hopes
that something more beautiful will come forward.

Until I look down at hands covered in my own blood
and realize that I am so terribly guilty

of silencing the parts of myself
screaming to be heard.

Consequences of Silence

A love left unrequited.
A poem left unfinished.
An argument that doesn't end in,
"I love you, I'm sorry."

A daughter left wondering
when it will ever be enough.
The disappointed pause after,
"Aren't I enough?"

A heart holding onto every one of its beats
to learn how to feel again.

Silence has hurt me
more than it has ever healed me.

But maybe what keeps me coming back
is that silence asks nothing of me.
Does not want for anything
other than a place to rest on my tongue.

In the moments when grief and anger
play puppet master with the strings of my heart,
silence tells me I do not have to rage.

Do not have to break if I do not want to.
They need not know how fragile I really am.
How all the broken pieces of myself
want to shatter into a million more.

Silence tells me
it will wrap around my vocal cords
before anyone can play me for a fool again.

But if silence were to step aside,
it would be because it knows
my words carry more weight than it ever could.

It would be to tell my lover
how much I truly adore him.
It would be because
the end of a poem came bursting
through the seams of my mouth, ready

to be heard in all its unrepentant existing.
It would be to tell my parents
that I am enough for all of us.

It would be because the rhythm of my heart
became a song I could sing to again.

Because no *"I'm sorry"*
could ever be worth more
than an *"I love you."*

When silence steps aside,
it is to make room for my laughter
finding home in the corners
of every desolate space.

To express my gratitude
for every unwavering shoulder of support.

For every soul that tells me it is okay to shatter
if I'm willing to mend again –

for who can dare make a fool
out of someone who always speaks their truth.

Haikus for the Starving Writer

artist by nature
leave room for no confusion
feel first, then create

a thousand voices
amplified through your courage
silence will not do

there is nothing small
about how you choose to live
fearlessly, with faith

in oceans of joy,
grief, everything in between
you must keep swimming

Altar

I come to my journal, weeks later,
a humble stranger once again.

Leave my pride at the door,
and try my best to shed my ego like an old skin,
ready to grow into something more fitting.

I lose who I am in the real world and come here
believing I will find it in my words instead.

Turn these pages into an altar
and leave pieces of myself as an offering,

a promise –

that I will live only with integrity in my voice.
With grace in my heart.
With kindness in my hands.

Hoping that it turns every broken part of me
into a poem instead.

The Becoming of a Poem

I am sipping on my mother's home brewed *chai*
when the newest metaphor for my melancholy
whispers in my ear.

Continues quietly along the canal leading to my mind
where it starts spinning symphonies in circles,

so, I set my cup down on the sill of my window
and reach for one of the only journals
I've managed to fill with half ideas and broken analogies.

Linger at the top of the page with an intention, a thought
that I must get this line out before anything else.

It takes a second to start, a minute to move,
as I begin to question if I even know
how to write a poem anymore.

When my pen touches the paper, I write carefully.
Shape out the curve of every letter as if
this is the only time poetry can ever be beautiful.

I try to remember not to think
for more than a few seconds between each sentence.

Remember that my hands know the words
I'm looking for even if my mind hasn't pieced it together
well enough just yet.

When the end of my page
looks considerably messier than the beginning,
imagery painting the pages the colors of all my secrets,
I know –

I've unearthed what I was looking for.

For the Shepherd Who Is Also the Path
the Sun Makes in Daytime
erasure poem after Komal Mathew

a wonder in contrapposto, an artist

without   burning

on an altar of choices.

a creator in the wild
becomes prey.

because no one ever writes
a love poem for the poet.

I often think of how bittersweet it is
that a poem is only ever allowed to be itself once.

and about how every time we come back to it,
it is with a different craving on our tongues,
a new comfort to draw from its words.

there's something powerful
in how no poem has ever turned me away.

in how each one took hold of my heart
in its hands and accepted it only as it was.

joyous, broken,
sometimes head over heels in love –
sometimes believing love did not exist at all.

gratitude seems too small for all the poets
who have housed echoes of my voice within their own,

even smaller in these hands that have yet
to give back as much as they've given me.

and yet, I still try.

every inch of these unstained pages
feels like miles of untraveled roads
when I find myself with a pen

between my fingers over and over again.

each time looking for a new way
in which I too can say to the next person,

"I see you.

  I hear you.

    I love you."

Ode to Babel
for Sarah Kay

Shivering under a lone string of fairy lights,
my best friend perched by my left shoulder,
faces as wide eyed and excited as mine
wait for the woman we all came to see.

A wordsmith of the most wondrous kind,
a testament to the talent found no further
than the heart of Brooklyn.

There is a gentle lull in the air,
our bellies full and our bodies lazy after her mother's
fresh baked oatmeal chocolate chunk raisin cookies.

There is no hoard of cameras in the air,
clicking faster than the seconds that pass
in a feeble attempt to freeze time on a six inch screen.

There is only one mic, one collective
holding of the breath before she begins her first poem
and finishes with what we all hope won't be her last.

Every heart in the vicinity turns
from stranger into familiar friend in these minutes,
tied together by nothing but a shared love for a woman
waiting to wake the world with her words.

Dandelions

Do you remember how much easier it was
to believe in magic when we were younger?

To etch our wishes onto the wisps of a dandelion
and send it off into the winds with nothing but hope.

How brave we must have been
to open our hearts so fearlessly.

To believe that if we wanted something bad enough,
all the karmic forces in the universe
would come together to make it happen.

Ethereal

There's something powerful
in the way that she stands.

It's not the way that she stands,
but that she'll look you straight in the eye when she does.

No chance to turn away, no mask to hide behind,
to be anyone other than who you are
in that very moment.

Maybe that's what's so beautiful
about what she has to offer this world.

That by living in her truth,
so boldly, so unapologetically,

we have no other choice than to accept our own.

Cosmic Love

Kiss her once,
                    twice,
                              three more times.

Let her know that you refuse
to take the chance that it wasn't perfect.

If there's ever a day where she questions
the depth of your love,

then paint the galaxies across every inch of her skin.
Trace the constellations
across the expanse of her stomach

and remind her that she fills herself
with the universe with every breath she takes.
That her bones are made up
of the same dust as the planets

and the strength she refuses to believe she has
holds her upright even when she wants
to fall to her knees.

And when you pull her hand up
to press your lips to the back of her knuckles,

do not neglect to tell her that God Himself
carved perfection into her curves.
She is so very beautiful.

And if this is the only thing in this world
of which you could be certain is true,

then live every day to make sure
she knows this too.

Love Shows Up As

A wolf in sheep's clothing.

Sneaks up on you with the invitation
of warmth and comfort,

while its teeth find their way to your jugular,
and rest over your pulse, a silent warning
as if to say,

"You are mine now.
One wrong move and you will feel it."

Cupid's Misadventures

I lose myself often
in the coffee stained pages of a book drenched in love.

Find blushing daisies guiding me down
paths less traveled, towards a kind of romance
more compromising than those
that I have known so far.

Sometimes, I do not feel ready for it.

Do not think my arms can welcome another embrace
without flinching in fear of the cold after they leave.
Do not think I can offer my heart again,
and have it returned broken, bloody, and bruised.

I think Cupid must have made a mistake.
Lost a few of his arrows in misguided attempts
to hunt for my happiness and here I am now,
nursing wounds from weapons that were not his.

A Letter to My (Abusive) Ex-Boyfriend

Sometimes, if the night is quiet enough,
the ghost of my past with you comes to haunt me
from the foot of my bed.

Asks me not to forget –
to remember so vividly

what I learned love not to be.
And once again, without my consent,
you invade my senses.

I think of how you told me
that you could spell my name out
with the strings of your guitar,
smiled at me as you said
you would write a song for every letter.

I wonder if you knew that you were writing a requiem.
A goodbye to the girl I used to be before you,
to the girl I could have been without you.

You swore to me that you tasted forever on my tongue,
but I needed you to know
that you no longer fit on my palette.

Forever had been stripped of its sweetness
and left only a bite on my lips,
and I have never been the type of girl
to so easily abandon my sweet tooth.

I remember how you said
that you smelled home in the strands of my hair.
Used words prettier than me to bind my wrists to yours

and I wanted to tell you
that even gilded cages become a kind of prison.

You insisted you loved me.
Tried to leave proof in the black and blue
handprints around my arms,
and I couldn't find my words quick enough

to tell you that I did not want a love letter
written in my own blood.

Is it any surprise that I haven't been able
to hold myself together the same since?

I think of how you claimed
that you saw heaven in my eyes.
Were certain that life without each other
could only ever be hell.

But I doubt you know that after you,
I stopped believing in God for a while.

So, the next time I find myself at the grave
of all the things I have ever felt for you,
I remember, I remember, and I remember

that this is not love.

Undeserving

I give too much of my time to questioning my worth –
wondering if I've fallen into the pattern
of accepting less than what I deserve.

There's plenty that I excuse
in the name of love, friendship, family.

But maybe, I have to treat this heart like my child –
mother it, protect it
from those too lost in themselves to ever see me.

Nothing in this life offers me permanence,
and if this is a lesson I must learn through people,
then so be it.

I am teaching myself more about honesty.
About how to hold myself accountable
when shaky lines I have drawn in sand are crossed.

Do I believe that I don't deserve better?
Or do I believe that better might never come along?

Alternate Universe in Which I Am Unharmed by The Men I Do Not Love
after Olivia Gatwood

When the sandwich maker at the deli
across the street from my high school
insists on adding a serving of what he thought
was irresistible charm to the side of every breakfast,
I do not smile politely hoping it is the only thing
he'll give me that I haven't asked for.

Instead, I smear a saccharine smirk on my face
and wait for the soft traces of my girlhood
to tickle the self-disgust in his belly.
His goading grin turns into a humbled chagrin,
and he hands me my bagel, this time without asking
if I have a boyfriend to pay for it.

When I tell my partner of two years
that I am unhappy with the way he makes me feel,
he doesn't tell me that I should be grateful
anyone loves me at all.

He does not poke and prod at all the parts of me
he knows to be the most tender,
does not coat his lips with poison
when he tells me to kill myself.
When he says the world would be better off
without someone like me.

Instead, he utters the first apology of many,
and he means it.

When a man who lives on my block
stops me a few houses away from home,
he does not feel compelled to tell me
that he's admired watching me grow
from the time I moved into the neighborhood
at the budding age of eleven.

He does not ask if he can take me to the movies
to get to know me better.
There is no empty bottle of liquor in his hand
for me to keep a wary eye on.
Instead, he asks about my day,
keeps one hand on the leash of his pitbull puppy
and wishes me a pleasant rest of my evening.

Here, in this universe,
I do not have to think of how there is no line
between being too safe and too paranoid.

Instead, I walk home at night
with my headphones in, volume turned all the way up.
With my keys in my bag and not gripped
like a lifeline between my fingers.
With a smile to every stranger along the way,
knowing they will not say that I was asking for it.

fireflies

they say that

it's better to have loved and lost,

than to never have loved at all.

and I promise,

that until meeting you,

I used to agree.

**an incomplete guide
to healing a broken heart.
written by a broken-hearted girl.**

one of the first things you learn about relationships
is that they come with heartbreak.

it hangs back in the corner like a jilted lover,
waiting for the day that one of you may trip
and fall in defeat instead of for the other.

sadly, there are no written guidelines
as to what you should do
when your heart feels emptier than your bed,
and your bed is just as empty as you.

so, here's what I've managed to put together so far.

one.

let it hurt.
the waves of sorrow in your chest
will inspire the tsunami in your eyes
but for now,
it is just about keeping your head above water.

the storm inside of you
will not quiet easily and, for a while,
you will feel like the tide of the ocean,
coming back to meet the sadness
you try so often to pull away from.

two.

breathe.
the first few days will be difficult.
you will wake up in the mornings
and have a rare moment of peace
before remembering.

and when you remember,
oh, it will hurt just like it did the first time.

your breath will get caught
in that junction between inhaling and exhaling
but keep in mind that, in that moment,

holding on to something
is more painful than letting go.

three.

isolate.
there is a fine line
between loneliness and solitude.
you must learn to take the former by its hand
before finding comfort in the latter.

pick up the pen, dip the brush in color,
and rediscover the things
that lighten the burden on your soul.

four.

fall out of love.
this, for me, has proven to be the hardest so far.

my days are spent teaching myself
to no longer whisper his name as a mantra
in the intervals between each heartbeat.

the moon does not bear witness
to our starlit conversations anymore,
but rather looks on in concern
as I have more talks with mary jane instead.

five.

I do not know what five is.

all I know is that every so often,
while I'm getting dressed in the morning,
my hands come across the shirt I stole
to stay warm on my way home once.

his scent has long since faded but, I swear,
I can press my nose to the fabric

and feel my heart break
all over again.

An Unfinished Love Story.

In the years it took me to find you,
I picked up every beautiful thing I saw along the way,
sewed it over my heart, and hoped
that the jagged edges from each heartbreak before
seemed a little less daunting.

In a world like this,
a love like mine is not meant to survive.

This love is every Saturday morning
spent in an unmade bed, sheets rumpled
with the promise of an unspoken invitation.
It's each excuse for being late
tucked underneath the pillow that smells like you.

This love is every August afternoon
lazing on your little balcony in Queens,
with Mary Jane curling her toes between us
until the sun begins to set.
Like the day could not stretch out long enough
for all the things we wanted to share.

My time with you finished before this poem could,
and while a part of me feels like
I should apologize for that,

I am learning not to ask forgiveness
for the things that have changed me.

I welcomed you into my little universe,
carried for you a warmth in my heart
that sweetened my world,
and strung your name between each beat
like prayer beads.

How fitting that in love I found religion,
when it is all I have ever looked for.

But I could not continue
to open my hands in supplication
and have it mistaken for an offering instead.

I still carry your name with me,
tuck it neatly into a jar of bittersweet memories,
and every now and again,
when a whisper of your ghost settles over my shoulders,

I remind myself
that love is one friend with many faces.

And though it may never wear yours again,
I remember you with only gentle hands and a soft hope
that you think of me just the same.

Bittersweet Lullaby

my heart breaks in the sweetest way

    every time you say my name,

knowing I'll never hear a sound

    this kind of beautiful again.

Almost

I still remember the time we first met.
You reminded me of the first time I tasted scotch.
It left me heady, heart beating,
like this was the kind of moment to live for.

Unfortunately, scotch also left me
with a head that felt ready to shatter,
a parting gift for the morning after,
like the moments worth living for all came at a price.

We were almost there.

Do you know the worst part about the word *almost?*
It's the idea that somewhere along the way,
something wasn't enough.
And the worst part about almost with me
is that somewhere along the way,

I felt like I wasn't enough.

It shouldn't have hurt the way it did
if we were only ever an almost.

When you walked out of my life so carelessly,
I almost didn't cry.

My chest tightened, my lungs burned,
and I almost couldn't breathe.

My heart ached,
and I almost couldn't take it anymore.

Maybe *almost* is supposed to hurt.

Because the next time I hear your name in passing,
I feel my heart break just a little bit more before I think,

"Oh. I almost forgot about him."

A Letter to My Revolving Door Lover

I wonder if you leave the door open just a crack
so it's easier for you to slip back in
without making too much noise.

> I stopped making your side of the bed
> knowing that there are nights
> when you stumble your way back to my side.

It's easy to ignore the taste of indifference
on your tongue when your hands are insisting
that I matter.

> When you roll me onto my back and let me feel
> how much you want me,
> God, how easy it is to believe
> that you want all of me.

You leave landmarks on the valley of my neck,
as if you need a roadmap to find your way back to me.

> I listen for the way
> my name used to slip past your lips like a prayer
> and find that your new favorite word is *fuck*.

Fuck.

> The red you left on my neck fits right in
> with the black ink in my skin
> and yet I must remind myself

that it should never be this difficult
to find your way back home.

It makes me want to write you out of my life,
so I start with changing the sheets on my bed.

When your scent no longer lingers,
I think with a clearer head.

If heartache is the only thing you bring with you,
then I'd rather have dinner alone
than set the table for two.

You make me ache in ways that make me feel
as though my bones are hollow.
How else can this sadness echo in the way that it does?

I seek solace in the arms of a friend
I know won't judge.

You see, Mary Jane has this profound ability
to lift me high when my heart sinks low.

She holds my hand while I close the door behind you,
and suddenly it becomes easier to breathe
when your shortcomings no longer fall on my shoulders.

I stand tall in the sun and find myself
filling with hope again.

I hope you look for my warmth
in the next girl you put your arms around.

I hope you see my coffee brown in her eyes
when she looks at you with unbounded admiration.

I hope you press your nose to the nape of her neck
and smell everything but my comfort.

When you work to remember the map
you left on my skin
and find yourself back at my doorstep, searching
for the home I wanted to be for you –

I hope you find that I've long since changed the lock.

Dear Mr. Nice Guy,

Who the fuck do you think you are?

It's so easy for you to come to your friend
and tell him about how you eased into her life
and then eventually into her.

You come to me and tell me
all about the endless curve on her body
but apparently, I'm supposed to curve the guy
who asked me out at the last open mic.

You know what I think it is?
I think it kills you to see a woman
who's not as scared of herself as you are of her.

The woman who glows
in her unapologetic confidence,
her unbridled intelligence,
her unabashed significance.

Let me tell you what we like.

We like the men who turn our names
into reverent prayers and mantras
because they see God in us.

The men who strip us down to our very core
before they even think about taking off our clothes.

We like the men who let us cum first
because we come first and it's never too fast
because these men always finish last.

I don't want your two minutes of love
and I definitely don't need your two seconds of lust.

You think I have a problem
with a forever type of commitment
but baby, I have seven instances of ink on my skin
that say otherwise.

I wear forever on my hips
like my favorite pair of denim jeans,
so, fuck you for thinking they look better on her
than they do on me.

There's no solid end to this piece
because there was no proper beginning with you.
And somewhere along the middle,
I realized this and I think you should too,
that maybe, just maybe,

you're not a nice guy after all.

Epiphany

In the days after you left,
there were times when I sprang out of bed
with a skip in my step for no particular reason.

I'd grab the first pair of comfortable pants I see
and pull them on before realizing
that I wanted to wear a dress instead.

My hair wouldn't quite smooth out the way
I would've liked for it to, but the wild curls matched
the freedom that now coursed through my veins.

I'd look in the mirror and notice that when I smile,
all my harsh edges and angles seemed to soften out,
and for just a second, I'd let myself think,

"Maybe I am beautiful."

But see, when you left,
you took the dead weight of the word *maybe* with you
and suddenly the burden of all my unmet expectations
fell from my shoulders.

I stained my lips with the very red you hated
and decided I was nothing short of a masterpiece.

I learned to like the way my smile curved higher
on the left side of my face.

I walked the roads you were too scared to travel
and found pieces of myself

tucked between pages of an unread book,
wedged into the lyrics of an unheard song,
perched on the seat before an unseen wonder.

And when I laid all these fragments out before me,
each piece seemed to seamlessly fit with the next.

I found order in all my chaos.
And now when I look in the mirror,
the word *maybe* does not precede the thought
that I am beautiful.

Before You Love a Poet
after Shivani Manohar

Before you love a poet,
or perhaps, before you love this poet,
realize that there's no way around it —
I have to write about you.

But please understand that on most days,
my words play hide and seek with me,
so, take every poem about you for exactly what it is —
a goddamned miracle.

You'll notice early on
that metaphors are my love language,
so, before I ever tell you that I love you,

I will confess instead that the beat of my heart
has started to sound a lot like your name.

Before you love a poet,
and that is to say, before you love this poet,
know that I will also write to you.

On the nights that you lay asleep beside me,
I will trail my fingers across your ribs
and leave you love letters written in braille.

When you wake up and find
that I've signed each with a kiss,
remember that I have only ever worn truth on my lips.

But if you smile and leave remnants
of your laughter between my sheets,
I hope you'll forgive me
if I do not send them back right away.

Before you love a poet,
and more importantly, before you love this poet,
please appreciate that despite how
I have left it vulnerable by doing so,
I still wear my heart on my sleeve.

Leave it at your mercy every time
I turn my palm up to meet yours,
and hope that you remain unafraid
of this kind of honesty, of this kind of love.

So if you choose to love a poet,
and really, I mean if you choose to love this poet,
do so if you can accept that this is all that comes with it.

I will write to you and about you,
but only ever with sincerity.

I do not know how else to love.

Melodies in Melancholy

I've been dating this guy who somehow ended up
charming an invitation out of me
to one of my open mics.

Suddenly, I have a stomach full of butterflies,
and I haven't been able to figure out
how they snuck their way in.

I've already laid in bed with him.
but fuck, is it so much more terrifying
to be naked in this way.

There's plenty that I've kept hidden, childhood secrets
tucked underneath my left shoulder blade.

Too bad it twitches whenever I perform.

It is a different kind of feeling
to bare my soul in front of someone I know.
Can't stop myself from hoping
for a radical kind of acceptance.

What does it say about me that acceptance
is all I have ever needed on most days?

Accept that a poet is all I know how to be?

I turn my melancholy into melody,
make symphonies out of the sorrow in my poems

when I perform and remember to hold happiness
in my hands to pass out as a *"thank you for listening."*

It gets too hard to breathe from under the layers of grief
that line the insides of my favorite sweaters,
so, I have learned to strip myself naked in front of those
who have the courage to keep looking me in the eye.

My mother says that this is very unladylike of me.
Tells me that no one would want a woman
brazen enough to pry open her ribcage to the world
and leave her heart on display.

She does not understand that
I do not want to be wanted otherwise.

When It Arrived
erasure poem after C.L. O'Dell

what I thought could save me.

was disappearing.

until you heard me.

Color Me Intrigued

If roses are indeed red, and violets are somehow blue,
then it must be true that I want you.
But is it true you want me too?

I have no name for this feeling you leave me with,
but the purple haze of my mind after you smile at me
limits my capacity for words anyway.

If I tell you my tongue is bubblegum pink,
does it tempt you to taste me?
I want to know if you'll find that comfort smells a lot
like my orange flavored lip balm.

I've been told more than once
that I inherited my father's green thumb,
and on some days, I want nothing more

than to grab a hold of this yellow tulip
I've planted by your name in my heart,
turn it into a bouquet and offer it to you in hopes
that you'll have me as a friend if nothing more.

But I make the mistake of looking into your brown eyes
and suddenly, things are no longer so black and white.

You bring color into my world artfully enough
to render a poet like me speechless.

That has to mean something
...doesn't it?

Weary in Wonderland

I'm standing at the verge of a familiar rabbit hole,
entrance lined alluringly with red roses
strung together with sweet words.

I wonder what the Mad Hatter will say this time.
"So, my darling, come to fall in love again?"

I'll smile and shake my head no,
even as my mind recollects on the feeling
of my hands in your hair,
of safety tucked against your chest.

I'll tell myself that I've taken this journey before
and that the novelty of all the tourist attractions
have worn off.

But the colony of butterflies in my stomach
are disconnected from the musings of my mind
and take no heed of my subconsciously conscious denial.

Fluttering wings leave a storm in my belly
every time you smile at me,
and I come just a little bit closer to falling from the edge.

Reasons to Love You

Because once you bought me a green tea
when what I really order from Starbucks is a Jade Citrus.

Because even though you got that part wrong,
you still remembered that I want
just one packet of honey.

Because you rarely ever use my name,
but every time you do,
I want to kiss it off your lips.

Because the sound of my name in your voice
will always remind me why I believe in music.

Because I haven't figured out how to laugh at something
without wanting to share it with you
immediately afterwards.

Because when I tell you what I think
are some of my funniest jokes, you like to pretend
that you don't find me so impossibly charming.

Because you refuse to sit across from me
in any restaurant –
instead, you wait for me to take my seat
before squeezing in next to me,
no matter how tiny the booth.

Because as we talk, one of your hands find their way
to the top of my knee in between warm bites of comfort,
and I am surprised yet again by how safe I always feel.

Because you cry to the same Jorja Smith songs that I do,
understand that this life is incomplete
without a little bit of heartbreak.

Because you look at me like I am the poem –
like you know all the secrets hidden between the lines.

Because you haven't yet given me a reason not to.

The Intimacy Of
after Felix Davis

Asking them if they already ate. Meeting them with a
chai latte in hand. Knowing which side of the bed they
enjoy. Having a nickname that is theirs only. Writing a
poem for them. Sending them only a single heart emoji
on the days that talking is too much. A random and
gentle kiss, etched onto any open area of their skin.
Handmade gifts from them, love stitched into the
intention. Buying them their first plant. Resuscitating
their first plant. Creating quietly next to them, relaxed in
being around good energy. Shared smiles in silent
conversation, no words needed for everything their eyes
say.

Curious About You

When they ask me to tell them about you,
I chuckle and say, *"Well, where do I begin?"*

I think of mentioning how
you are constantly moving towards the life
that you deserve, the life that you've earned.

About how you turn every failure into a lesson,
change every rejection into redirection,
accept every success as a blessing.

I want to talk about how you've made this world
into just another mystery to be understood.
And how the spark in your eye shines brighter
when you start to connect one puzzle piece to the next.

But I want to keep to myself the smirk
that finds its way to your face when you're talking
about all the boundaries you run into.

Like it's so funny that life thinks
it can just hold you back.

If I don't, I'll have to admit
that every victory that inspires your most genuine smile
makes me feel like there is nothing
that cannot be achieved if I have you within my reach.

Fall From Grace

There's something to be said for the look in your eyes
when you catch my gaze and tell me that you want me.
Dangerous in its honesty, inviting in its admission.

Did you mean to kiss this secret into my mouth?

The curve of your lips follows the line of my neck,
and I want to know if you'll familiarize yourself
with every part of my body this way.

I get my answer when your hands ghost over my skin,
fingers trailing like sentences that can never be finished.

Warmth blooms underneath where you touch
just a little more,
and I can't catch my breath quick enough
to tell you to keep going.

But you know, don't you?

Know how to stain my skin in red
to mirror the ink in yours.
Your hand snakes around my neck,
tightening like this knot in my stomach.
Bruising kisses littered along my collarbone
reads like a love letter full of promises.

Fuck, what a heady feeling –
to know I'm safe in the face of your primal need

to take my breath away.

You can't stop tasting, and I can't stop from falling.
A whisper in the back of my mind wonders

if this is how Lucifer felt when he was cast from heaven.

For how salacious it feels to call out for God,
when you burn your smile into my inner thigh,
mischief in your eyes,

intent on making a sinner out of me.

Sleepy Saturdays

The rain leaves me sleepy, in ways
that make me want for your lips pressed against
the spot behind my ear.

For the way the drops of water
hide the sound of happiness that slips out
of my hummingbird heart.

A contented sigh as my fingers flex and curl
around the curve of your bicep, stubborn
against admitting that I'd like you so much closer.

The rain makes me want to tuck my face
into the crook of your neck, the smell of your skin
so beautifully human in the humidity.

Run my hand along the back of your shoulders,
fingers coming up to play in your hair, a silent pleasure
in how you lean into me even more.

Pull your hips flush against mine,
an underlying tension beneath this craving
to just be near you.

The rain makes me want to break all the clocks
in your house, every passing second a reminder
that this moment is fleeting, just like the rest.

Makes me wish you'd smile and pull me outside
to dance in the storm, like we used to
when we were young –

like we're not still just two crazy kids
who found someone to be crazy with.

Unravel Me

I find it hard to get you out of my mind.
Shared moments so sinful despite the tenderness,
I'm surprised my cheeks don't burn me where I stand.

I can't keep conversation and pretend
like it's not your voice I want in my ear instead,
quiet whispers making me feel something
in the way only you can.

I am always bringing myself back
to the present moment, away from the edge of insanity
you love to push me to.

But if they were watching close enough,
they would see the ghost of your hands
leaving a forest of goosebumps along my spine,

roadmaps of all the different ways
you've caused my unraveling.

Compass

I've often looked for comfort in the crook of your neck.
Learned to leave my worries near the coat rack
by your doorstep and wait for your hands
to invite me into safety.

When I press my nose against your skin
and whisper prayers into forbidden flesh,
I ask God only for you.

Ask that He see how your heart
has become my anchor, grounding me,
when storms around me leave my feet unsteady.

Ask that He hear how my name falling from your lips
has become the sound of my true north – an invitation,

calling me home, every time

I am lost.

Realize

I'm not sure I could tell you when I knew.

It snuck up on me slow enough
to make me unable to remember a time
that I didn't love you.

I climb the stairs up to your room,
tempted by the lull of warmth I always find
between your covers.

Your eyes take their time
getting to know all of me again, a small smirk
playing on your lips as I fidget in indulgent nervousness.

You say hello only when I smile back,
lower my shoulders just enough to know that I am safe.

Make your way to me surely,
with steps bigger than my breath at having you
this close to me again,

and when your arms twist around my waist to pull me in,
I can't help the surprise
in how my body recognizes yours already.

One hand tracing along the nape of your neck,
the other wrapped around your shoulders
like I'd finally learned what it means
to lean on somebody.

Your own hands travel up my back,
a familiar journey for you by now
as you turn your face in to tickle
the underside of my jaw with your beard.

Smiling kisses travel up the valley of my neck
before resting for a second longer
on the blush of my right cheek,
and a small hum slips past my lips.

Your arms tighten around me
just the slightest bit in response,
as if to promise you wouldn't let go.

As if to say you already know.

Confession

Last week, I took a chance
and finally whispered in your ear that I love you.
Admitted that I only didn't want to tell you
because I needed to be absolutely sure

I would not regret giving these precious words away.
I did not want them returned to me
with a gentle *no, thank you.*

Last week, I confessed to you that the beat of my heart
has started to sound a lot like your name.

And when my tongue stuttered over this secret,
you grinned at me in endearing amusement.
Asked if I was scared that you wouldn't love me back.

I thought for a second –
surprised myself with the honesty behind my *no.*
You don't have to say it for me to know.

It's evident in the way you touch your lips
against the racing pulse of my temple when I'm anxious.

And the way your hands hold onto mine like an anchor
when I am struck with the urge to run from myself.

It's in the stillness of the silence shared
after a moment of vulnerability.

You do not have to say it for me to know.

So, when you ask if I am scared and I say no,
I mean it.

With you, there is nothing to be afraid of.

To My Last Love

Most mornings, you'll probably sneak out of bed
before I do to make me coffee
in the best way you know how,

but I promise that when you least expect it,
I will surprise you with breakfast first instead.

It's customary to start the day off with something sweet,
or at least that's what my mom says,

so, I promise that I will not let you
take a bite of the pancakes without kissing
last night's dreams off your lips first.

I might be a little cranky some days,
even anxious enough to ask if you still like me.
And, I mean, yeah I know you love me,
but liking isn't really the same thing?

Last love, I promise it's not you that I'm doubting,
it's just my own inability to believe
that I could deserve something this kind of wonderful.

I want to make you feel wonderful,
so, I promise that on the nights that you don't,
I will pluck the stars from the sky to surround you with.
Remind you that there is no universe for me
without you in it.

When cupid found me and reassured me
of the gentle way your hands would hold my heart,
I did not hesitate to unstitch it from where I've worn it
on my sleeve for the last few years.

When God Himself told me that your name
would be another prayer falling off my lips,
I recited all the hymns I knew to make space
for the last one I'd ever need.

I wanted you to be mine
with as much certainty as I know
the moon belongs to the night sky,
and I closed my eyes to dive into this heart first.

So, last love, I promise, it's not you that I'm doubting.
It's just my own inability to believe
that I could deserve something this kind of wonderful.

Even Bees Know What Zero Is
erasure poem after Christian Wimin

That's enough memories, thank you,

I had to pay for that,
and in currency quite other than attention.
I've had my fill of truth, too,

Live long enough, and

That's the bad news.
The good news? You don't give a shit.
My life. It's like a library that

              opens only to an improved confusion:
theology where poetry should be,

And I'm all the regulars
and   the   disciplines too.
But most of all I'm

one more thing I'm done with

Blue Is the Warmest Color

I have lived
in so many different moments of blue.

From the worn down denim
of my favorite oversized jacket,
to the petals of forget-me-not flowers
from lovers left in the past.

Sitting next to roaring oceans reflecting cloudless skies,
dipping brushes in watercolors that stain my canvas
enough to hide the tears that fell first.

And when I draw myself into the picture,
I trace my heart in shades of cerulean.

So when people ask me how I'm feeling,
I stay silent

and point to the part of my body
that is permanently painted in heartbreak.

Armchair Psychology

Somewhere between stuffing my depression
into a pillowcase and making a puppet of my anxiety,
I am expected to read three chapters
on behavioral psychology.

As if Watson or Pavlov could ever make sense
of why I believe more in my potential for failure,
than my ability to make a lesson of it.

As if it would allow me to reach my hands up
and find where the faith in myself
had fallen from my crown.

As if it should explain how on most days,
my own mind is my very worst enemy.

Diagnosis
after Andrea Gibson

I suffer from Overly Apologetic Syndrome.
Sorry, I actually think it's called
Can't Stop from Being Sorry Syndrome.

I'm always apologizing in between my sentences.
like I'm expecting to be chastised
for having said something to begin with.

I say sorry at the start of an open mic performance
if I end up sharing a repeat poem,
because really, who wants to hear me
say the same thing more than once?

I say sorry at the end of a long winded journey
of one of my thought processes
that turn every conversation into a rollercoaster.

Say sorry when I catch the other person looking at me
in amused indulgence, because that was more
of their time than I meant to take up.

I say sorry when I feel like I need to explain
being the way that I am.

Sorry, I think I meant to say I say sorry just for being.

de·pres·sion (n.)

When my best friend asked me to define my depression,
my first thought was to grab the nearest Webster
and read off the given definition.

"A state of feeling sad," it said.

The meaning had fallen short of the feeling so instead,
I told her about the way my lungs
would sometimes detest the taste of air,
and the strength it took to remind myself
that I needed it.

There were times when my limbs felt heavy enough
to leave me sinking into my mattress,
and I'd wonder if the stones that Virginia Woolf carried
as she walked towards her last breath
somehow found their way into my hands instead.

I used to think that the aroma of my mother's house
was a marriage of spices that she carried as comfort
in the pockets of her apron,
but the day depression first took my hand in its own,
I learned that most marriages end in divorce anyways.

Depression was never just feeling sad.

Depression was sometimes not feeling at all.
It was sometimes feeling everything at once.

It was the monster underneath your bed
that found its way into your head,
while the people around you stayed adamant
that monsters did not exist.

But this monster existed.

When my best friend asked me
how it felt to have conquered depression,
I told her that conquering it would have meant
that it was gone for good.

Instead, I locked it safely behind bars
just wide enough for it to sneak through
on the nights it could be stealthy enough to do so.

My depression does not leave me.

It stands by my side on my worst days
and follows me as a shadow on my best.
She asks if I feel wiser for having gone through it,
for continuing to go through it.

I tell her,
there is no wisdom to be found in grief this heavy.
No knowledge worth the well of tears I use
to water myself into the next day.

I tell her,
I just want to rest.

status update
after Rebecca Lindenberg

4/9/2021
8:46 p.m. | brooklyn, ny

khaotic is mind-numbingly exhausted –
trying to take the lead out of her limbs
to pick herself back up.
is digging through her closet for a shirt
that doesn't flatter her sadness.

khaotic is reminiscing
about the last breakfast that she enjoyed.
questioning if she will ever convince her mind
that her body is a friend and not a foe.
is watering every living thing in her room but herself.

khaotic is buying yet another planner
to fill with all the tasks
that her depression will never let her finish.
left wondering when she has made a lover
out of her nihilism.

is trying so hard to believe that just trying is enough.

khaotic is missing her chosen family.
is a black belt in breaking her own heart.
is somehow still waiting to be kissed again.

khaotic is dancing in the rain
to see if God's tears feel heavy like her own.
wants to steal colors from the rainbow after
to add to the blue smeared across her ribs.
because really, khaotic wants not to feel this lonely.

khaotic just wants not to feel this alone.

Cup of Tea

Sorrow stands on my doorstep like an uninvited friend,
toeing my welcome mat with the tip of her scuffed boot.

Maybe it is the familiarity of the gesture that brings me
to take her hands in mine and invite her in
for a cup of tea.

The blush of her oversized sweater only calls my eyes
to the lack of color in her cheeks.
And suddenly, I feel too exposed
in my oversized t-shirt and shorts.

I wonder if she sees that the touch of her blue
doesn't stain my wrists anymore.

When we knew each other better, I used to sleep
with my door unlocked and the hallway light on,
just in case she needed somewhere
safe to spend the night.
Somewhere familiar.

These days, I turn the knob on both locks of my door
and make sure all the lights have been turned off
before climbing into the comfort of my bed.

The first night Sorrow knocked on my door.
Loud, abrasive, unapologetic
about the late-night intrusion.

The second night, she knocked once more.
Rhythmic, gentle, remorseful
of yesterday's behavior.

The third night, she knocked once
and then left me alone.

I look at her now
with my grandmother's china warming her hands,
and recognize how far apart
we've grown from each other.

She sees the awareness in my face and smiles at me,
a somber acceptance in the quirk of her lips —

kisses my cheek with the promise
of once a month postcards instead of daily visits,
and wishes me to be happy until then.

Lines for the Fortune Cookies
after Frank O'Hara

resilience is a painful virtue. soften your stance.
bow your head as often as you need to.

stop. breath in…hold…breath out.
release the tension in your shoulders.
repeat as needed.

you are here to create your own belonging.

all the joy and light you deserve is on its way to you.

remember little you. honor little you, always.

write every poem that finds its way out of you.
including the bad ones. especially the bad ones.

hug your friends. tell them they've taught you family.
love them like they always forget just how much.

say good morning to your plants every day –
they are here to teach you how to grow.

smile at least once a day and learn
to find simple beauty in the mundane.

end every night with a breath of gratitude
for all the good things in your life –
and remember to include yourself.

Butterfly Effect

I couldn't tell you when she arrived,
only that she was there when I opened my eyes.

Striking sunset wings moved in sync with my breath,
every wave setting off a tornado
in someone else's stomach.
Wiry lines of black running over her body, broken
like one too many promises from the wrong person.

The sounds around me dull down,
and it becomes only her and I existing in one moment.

I wondered what called her to me.

Did the still mending pieces of my heart shimmer
against each other like wind chimes?
Could she see me trapped in the chrysalis
of my own mind, struggling
to let my wings breathe in fear of disrupting the air.

I watched as she sat perched on top of my shoe,
no care in the world for every storm started
by her dancing wings,

and wondered
if I could ever have the courage to do the same.

I Am Here Because

This grief that I have been carrying
has found a way to anchor itself around my ankles.

Turned my tears into an ocean
I am continually trying to wade through,
trying not to let my sadness make a landmark out of me.

A broken compass in hand, no true north
to point me back home to myself.
To the seven year old me, curled up and hiding
in the ruins of my own heart.

I've only ever wanted to come back home to her.

The girl that had to trade
playground swings for hospital hallways.
The one who gave her mother to her little brother
and is still trying to keep herself warm at night.
The one who lost her voice in a family
full of constant noise.

I am here because there is a story to tell,
and my voice now carries all the cadences
of the girl I used to be before I became
the woman I am now.

I am here because she deserved better.
I am here because I deserve better.

Ways in Which I Remain Strong

I brew a cup of *chai* using my mother's recipe –
remember her warmth with every sip,
and let it soften the stone this world tries
to turn my heart into.

Remind myself that nothing that is growing
is meant to survive in the cold.

I breathe through the tremors
of my never steady hands and wait until
my fingers are certain enough to roll flowers
into a bouquet.

Bring flowers with me to open mics
on the nights that I still crave community.
Keep one in my hands every time I reach out
to someone else, and marvel

at how blessings arrive when you continue to offer
the very best parts of yourself in return.

I leave my worries at the door
and dare to laugh in the midst of my heaviest grief.
Brave a smile despite the river of tears
that threaten to drown me if I do not learn
to keep my head above water.

And when I still feel the beginning cracks
in the foundation of who I am,

I turn my acceptance into a sledgehammer
and allow myself to break.

Little Pleasures

The beginning notes of my favorite song
from six years ago, a sweet pang in my belly
for the girl I used to be.

The drying petals on the roses
from my birthday bouquet – a reminder
that beauty never fades, it simply changes shape.

The soft lull of rainy days in busy cities.
Of slower mornings and languid *how are you's,*
where we take the time to ask – take the time to listen.

The sound of tiny sparrows, singing sonatas
even on brisk autumn mornings.
How the sun touches my mirror when it rises,
a gentle kiss as if to say,
"Look at yourself with kind eyes today."

The knot in my throat when I find myself
in my new favorite poem, metaphors mirroring
the parts of me I always assumed were too chaotic
to be understood.

How I've Managed to Stay Alive

When I start to unconsciously avoid
the mirrors in my house, I look myself in the eyes,
and I recognize what is not mine —

shed the shame I've inherited
from the women in my family,
and stand with my head held high, gold adorning
every part of the body I am supposed to hide.

The skeletons in my closet
rattle against the worn down wooden door,
so I bury secrets under similes
in every half written poem in my journal.

When they still insist on finding their voices somehow,
I turn my chaos into catharsis behind the microphone
of the most intimate open mics I can find.

I turn every poem into a performance,
by which I mean a prayer —

pray that someone sees me,

      hears me,

          loves me anyway.

15 things that lighten my heavyweight heart

i. the warm feel of my mother's hand brushing sadness away from the strands of my hair.

ii. a chocolate mister softee cone at almost any time of the year.

iii. the sound of my nephew's laughter when he finally gives in to my hugs, arms wrapped around him like I'd be able to keep him this happy forever.

iv. raindrops knocking on my window at night, the earth's reminder that sometimes God grieves in the same way that we do.

v. a thoughtfully curated playlist of all the songs that fill in for the beat of my heart when the music in my life dies down.

vi. smiles from my friends, the corners of their mouths teaching me how to reach up for the skies again.

vii. freshly laundered sheets and a warm blanket, because there are some things better dealt with from the comfort of my own bed

viii. hearing *"I love you."* not to me. just hearing it said, feeling it linger in the air and wanting the moment to last a little longer, because if there's something this world needs, it's a little bit more love.

ix. a bouquet of my favorite flowers. an ephemeral moment of beauty that says, *"I thought of you when I saw these."*

x.   an artfully rolled joint. flower mixed with
     lavender, a smooth burn to my relaxation.

xi.   the fact that my snake plant has grown so
      much with the least bit of attention from me,
      proof that some things must be left alone to
      flourish.

xii.   poems that see me with the very first line,
       offer me place to rest my heart, and let me
       know that all I must do here is be.

xiii.   the feel of his lips against my forehead.

xiv.   bowing into child's pose. feeling my heart
        melt against the ground and surrendering
        myself to the flow of the universe around me.

xv.   blurry polaroids. capturing only our naïve
      desires to hold onto the important moments
      for longer than they are meant to be held.

Right Now, I Need

Quiet. A morning far away in the mountains, but without any towers nearby lest someone assume I need saving. When my feet cross the threshold into solitude, I expect every hair on my body to finally lay flat where it had trembled in anticipation before. Where every moment became a holding of the breath, waiting for the shoe to finally drop. I wonder if my eyes will feel like they're opening for the first time without the usual cloud of anxiety hanging over me. Maybe I am just afraid to ask for this kind of quiet. To be left with my own mind, listening to the endless running of thoughts that make the inside of my head feel like a circus. I'm scared to walk across the tightrope holding the pieces of my sanity together, not knowing if the person I find on the other side will be someone I can learn to like – every quivering hand, every tremble of the voice, every uninterrupted thought. Maybe quiet does nothing but show me how learning to become never truly stops.

6:24 a.m.

she woke to the sound of the sky breaking,
hearing its echo resonate within
the cage of her ribs.

the dawn began with just a little bit of destruction,
a touch of chaos.

for just a second, she found comfort
in the way she could hook her thumbs
in the stretched-out sleeves of her worn-out sweater
and wrap her arms around herself.

perhaps that was the moment the broken pieces of her
started to come back together.

she felt warmth begin
at the very tips of her temples, subtle dips
on the sides of her head that rang louder
than a thousand bells on the nights
she could not find sleep.

it swam through her veins until it settled
for a minute around her right pinky finger,
bent ever so slightly where
all the empty promises had found a home.

it danced across her hips
to twirl on the third finger of her left hand,
now more naked than the soul she had bared

until, finally, she felt it curl
around the fluttering hummingbird in her chest.

and in moments like these,
when the sky mourns without abandon,
she is reminded that every now and again,

even the universe shatters.

Monday Morning Blues

When you open your eyes in the morning,
let your first conscious exhale leave your chest
in a rush of gratitude.

Get up and brush your teeth until
you've got a smile bright enough to convince everyone
you haven't spent your entire night crying.

Grind coffee beans into a roast bitter enough to sweeten
your tongue from yesterday's disappointments.

When your mother places your favorite breakfast
in front of you, let the *I love you* follow
the *thank you* that she deserves.

After you've filled your cup with enough water
for both you and your plants,
do not forget to turn your own face towards the sun.

If your planner taunts you from the top of your desk,
remind yourself that the only thing you must do
…is be.

For now, this is enough.

The Ocean Holds Me

Today, I found myself being pulled towards the ocean.
A quiet whisper I almost ignored, until
it became a restless knocking against my chest.

The train carries me towards the beach —
I can see the waves before I can hear them,
and a small part of my spirit seems to settle.

When I can smell the tide before I can see it
kissing the shoreline, the knocking in my chest
turns into a gentle thrum instead.

A hum of anticipation at being close
to something so much bigger than myself.

I walk to the edge of the waves,
and the water curls around the curve of my legs,
a sultry invitation to dive into the unknown.

So, I let the ocean hold me
as I release the tired in my weary bones.
Comfort me as I baptize myself of my grief,
and nourish me as I find my inner child underneath.

Every last worry washed away in another gentle reminder
of how ephemeral we truly are.

Sacrifices

On the nights my legs are locked in place,
and I feel unable to make it to the other side,
I have no choice but to leave behind everything
that threatens to hold me where I stand.

Every relationship that comes with a list of conditions,
the first of which asks me to give up my voice.
The constant guilt that I carry in my pocket
like a souvenir out of the vault of family heirlooms.

The idea that dreams as high in the clouds as mine
have no way to become a reality.
That words this heartbroken could have no space
in this world if the universe has already written
the poem I've intended on writing.

This aching part of my chest that wants nothing more
than to hear that everything will somehow be okay.
The innocent belief that I will always be accepted
if I stay honest with how I love –
eyes shut closed, heart wide open.

I'm trying my best to make it to the other side, a place
where happiness lives on the edge of discomfort,
only a few steps away from growth.

Where it's only myself that I romance,
it's only me that I love the way I've loved others.

Where I accept my evolution, understand that healing
is a gift and one that I am still wrapping today
to leave under my pillow.

Where I say goodbye to the things that do not serve me,
and abandon the companion I've made of my cynicism
to marry the flow of the universe instead.

To My Longest Lover Pt. II

I am in the middle of a California king bed,
curtains pushed to the side so I can watch
as the sun rises on the east along the west coast.

I collect each ray of light and pocket it for a rainy day,
knowing I can't delay the inevitable,
but I will try to make it sweeter.
I say good morning to the plants lining my windows
who need as much of this warmth as I do.

Head to my kitchen and sing at the top of my lungs,
my days of neglecting to nourish my body
left long behind in a house that never fed my spirit.
No longer out of tune with what I find fulfilling,
no guilt for indulging in the things that bring me joy.

And even this is just the beginning.
I haven't even started to romance myself yet.
Give myself flowers, fresh peonies for my dresser
every time there is a reason to celebrate myself –
and aren't there so many?

For the laughter I find blooming in my stomach
after a monsoon has passed through
the valley of my heart.

For the feeling of home I offer in my voice,
knowing how weary it gets searching
for a place to belong.

For every poem I pull out of my veins,
and every act of bravery that led me to it.

I have allowed too many of my journeys around the sun
to be revolved around other people,
those who never offer the same intention back.

So each day going forward
becomes a promise instead –

to forgive myself for the times I do not know better,
for the times I do not do better even if I do know.

To wrap my arms around my shoulders
and offer acceptance as a never ending gift.

To leave pockets full of love by the edge of my mirror,
a present to wake up to after a night
of convincing myself that I do not deserve it.

It seems like the very least I can do.

Grateful For

The deep belly laughs from my nephews, gleeful in their
innocence, not yet heart broken by this world. A tiny
spot on the shoreline only a few inches shy of the ocean
tide coming in, where I realize how small I truly am.
Cozy corners in Brooklyn that are just mine, where I've
named the plants I recognize and speak to the ones I
don't know yet. Sound checks at live music shows, a
secret smile shared between musicians in a moment that
is only theirs. Baristas who take the time to remember
my drink order and my name. Coffee shop poems that
taste like autumn, every word dipped in a nostalgic
longing for a warmer time. My mother's home brewed
chai, a recipe passed down from her mother, and her
mother before her. Scalp massages and amla oil
treatments that will always remind me of home. Cold
mangos as a midnight snack, sweet memories of summer
nights with my cousins. The rare occasion when all my
friends are free, and birthday brunches feel like family
gatherings. Picnics in hidden pockets of beautiful parks,
contentedness in just being together. Comfort in warm
plates of food, hands held under the table like a secret
that is only ours. Kisses on my forehead, a second to
close my eyes and lean in, allow myself to be cared for.
Spaces where I am safe enough to put my guard down,
trust that I will only be accepted. Communities that have
taken me in as one of their own. The lesson that I only
ever have to be better than I was yesterday, especially
when tomorrow is never promised. Trying my best to be
here today.

a woman like me.

in this life, there are those who know me
and those who love me, and I often wonder
if they are ever one and the same.

there are secrets I have wedged between my molars,
insecurities tucked beneath the curve of my hip bone,
trauma taped to the plate of my sternum.

my body has somehow become
a museum of my history.

I have never been comfortable
putting my pain on a pedestal.
my joy feels too sacred to share so freely,
but this world demands honesty of me –
knows that I will not exist
without giving it my voice.

so, I reach into the pit of my stomach
and find enough courage to tell you
that I am sun showers in March
and the first bloom of the spring.

I am a giver that has never learned to take.
give this heart to those with unsteady hands,
this smile to those who inspire rivers of tears,
this love to everyone but myself.

there are days when I feel
like I am made of origami paper.
it takes but one tug to pull me apart at my seams.

I fall victim to the whims of the moon,
find myself waxing and waning
like another unstoppable force of nature.

carry stardust in my pockets
for those who need a little magic to fill their days,

discover family in my friends
and finally understand
what *unconditional* means.

I learn to count my life in moments —
the ones that make me cry from happiness,
laugh until my stomach hurts,
love until my heart aches.

at times,
I question my commitment to this craft.
wonder if I am worthy enough

to be called a poet
if there are nights when my voice abandons me.

but time teaches me the way it always has,
and I begin to feel magic in my veins again.
start to pluck poetry out of the air in my lungs
and recognize that,

in truth, I am more prisoner than poet
with the way this pen holds me captive.

and after spilling my soul onto this paper,
the only thing left to ask is —
now that you know me,

can you dare to love a woman like me?

Glossary

I Begin

- Shavasana – corpse pose in modern yoga practice, a grounding practice meant for relaxation.
- Laal cha – translates to *red tea*, a Bengali black tea infused with ginger, cardamoms, cloves, and bay leaves for numerous health benefits.

kintsugi.

- Kintsugi – the Japanese art of repairing broken pottery by mending the areas with lacquer mixed with golden powder; honors the philosophy that breakage and repair are a part of an object's history, rather than something to be disguised.

11:11/make a wish

- Choto fufu – youngest paternal aunt.
- Boro fufu – elder paternal aunt.

কানিজ

- My given name written in Bengali, and my third tattoo inscribed over my lower left rib; a reminder to stop running from myself.

A Letter to Third Culture Children…
So, I Suppose, Another Letter to Myself

- Chai – traditional spiced tea blend; made with black tea leaves and occasionally mixed with strong spices, like cinnamon, cardamom, cloves.
- Salwar – a shortened reference to *salwar kameez*, a traditional attire for Bengali women.

Ancestry

- Dada – paternal grandfather.
- Dadu – paternal grandmother.
- Paan – betel leaf, often chewed with betel nuts and other spices for their stimulant effects; a pastime heavily practiced in South Asia.
- Sari – a traditional garment for South Asian women; a long stretch of stitched/embroidered fabric draped around the body in a variety of ways.
- Roti – a round, soft, and chewy flatbread.
- Bismillah – a shortened reference to the Arabic phrase *Bismillah Hir Rahman Nir Rahim*; translates to *In the name of God, the Most Gracious, the Most Merciful* – one of the most important phrases in Islam and used by Muslims before starting good deeds or before beginning most daily actions.
- Lassi – a South Asian beverage; traditionally a blend of mango, milk, and yogurt.

Dichotomy

- Aloo bhazi – a South Asian take on home fries; traditionally cooked with onions, tomatoes, Thai chili peppers, cilantro, and your choice of additional vegetables.

Pearls of Wisdom

- Sunnah – traditions and practices of the prophet Muhammad (peace be upon him) that constitute a model for Muslims to follow.

Mornings with Ma

- Thaffa – a wide, slightly curved in skillet used to make roti.

Hello, God? It's Me, Khaotic.

- Adhaan – Arabic word meaning *to listen*; the Islamic call to prayer, often recited by an Imam five times a day at the mosque.
  - o Imam – the person who leads prayers at the mosque; notably knowledgeable in Islam and well versed in the Quran.

Acknowledgements

First and foremost, I would like to thank you, friend.

Becoming an author, let alone a self-published one, always felt like a dream that was just out of reach. It is because of people such as yourself that it is now my reality instead.

I am forever grateful to you for supporting my poetry, for finding something in my writing you wanted to take home, and I am so beyond humbled by the thought that any poem of mine could be the one that makes you feel seen – because you absolutely deserve to be seen.

I want to thank my editors, Jahmadi, Nahrin, Ayesha, and Adam, without whom many of these poems would not have been loved into becoming. Thank you to Kristal, for working with me again and creating such a beautiful cover for this book.

And an enormous thank you to all my friends in the creative community who offered me unlimited encouragement, unconditional understanding, and invaluable insight throughout this journey.

I would not be here without any of you.

I hope that this book brings you home to yourself – that it gives you the courage to find your voice, and to bloom beyond your own boundaries.

Thank you, thank you, thank you.

About the Poet

Khaotic is a Brooklyn born poet finding her footing in New York City's creative community. As a brown woman coming from an immigrant and Muslim family, one of Khaotic's biggest goals as an artist has been to cultivates spaces for voices that often feel unheard. Through her brand and business, House of Khaos, she encourages communities of creatives to find confidence in their craft, and to find kinship in each other.

In February 2022, Khaotic published a limited-edition chapbook, *Plucking Petals of Poetry* – a project that came into the world as a teaser to her full-length manuscript, *Blooming Beyond the Boundaries*. When she's taking a breath from her love of poetry, you can find her in bookstores with her friends, watering any one of her twelve plants, or enjoying morning walks throughout her favorite parts of the city.

To keep up with the khaos, find Khaotic at

www.houseofkhaos.us

www.ingramcontent.com/pod-product-compliance
Lightning Source LLC
Chambersburg PA
CBHW011237120626
46549CB00009B/3306